SHACKLETON
THE SURVIVOR

Christine Butterworth

OXFORD
UNIVERSITY PRESS

OXFORD
UNIVERSITY PRESS

Great Clarendon Street, Oxford OX2 6DP

Oxford University Press is a department of the University of Oxford.
It furthers the University's objective of excellence in research, scholarship,
and education by publishing worldwide in

Oxford New York

Auckland Bangkok Buenos Aires Cape Town Chennai
Dar es Salaam Delhi Hong Kong Istanbul Karachi Kolkata
Kuala Lumpur Madrid Melbourne Mexico City Mumbai
Nairobi São Paulo Shanghai Taipei Tokyo Toronto

Oxford is a registered trade mark of Oxford University Press
in the UK and in certain other countries

Published in the United Kingdom
by Oxford University Press

First published 2001
10 9 8 7 6 5 4

British Library Cataloguing in Publication Data

Data available

ISBN 0 19 917448 2

Also available in packs

Explorers and Discoveries Inspection Pack (one of each book) ISBN 0 19 917452 0
Explorers and Discoveries Class Pack (six of each book) ISBN 0 19 917453 9

Acknowledgements

The Publisher would like to thank the following for permission to reproduce the following:

Photographs
Bridgeman Art Library/Scott Polar Research Institute, Cambridge: p 23; Corel Professional Photos: pp 10/11 (bottom), 20, 29;
Corbis/Eye Ubiquitous: p 22; Corbis/Peter Johnson: p 16 (both); Corbis/Wolfgang Kaehler: pp 4/5; Corbis/Rick Price: p 28;
Hulton Getty: p 5 (top); National Oceanic & Atmospheric Administration/Department of Commerce: p 19; Royal Geographical
Society: pp 9, 10/11 (top), 11 (right), 13 (both), 14, 15 (both), 17, 21, 30, 31

Front Cover: Royal Geographical Society

Back Cover: Hulton Getty

Quotations used are from the following copyright books:
p 15, p 17 and p 21 from Alfred Lansing: Endurance (Weidenfeld and Nicolson, 1999), pp 105, 116 and 193.
p 12, p 13, p 19, p 20, p 29 and p 31 from Ernest Shackleton: South (Robinson Publishing, 1998), pp 66, 77, 129, 158, 211
and 344.
p 4, p 22, p 24 and p 28 from F A Worsley: Shackleton's Boat Journey (Pimlico, 1999), pp 20, 170, 96 and 212.

Illustrated by Trevor Parkin and Matt Buckley
Designed by Alicia Howard at Tangerine Tiger
Printed in Hong Kong

CONTENTS

20th May 1916:

STROMNESS WHALING STATION, IN THE ANTARCTIC ...

Two small boys saw the three figures first. They were coming from the mountains where no human had ever been. The boys took one look and ran away, terrified. Were they human?

Long, filthy hair and beards hung round gaunt faces. Their skin was black with dirt and pitted with frostbite. Ragged, filthy clothes hung off them. They stank.

The manager of the whaling station came to the door of his hut. He stared. Who were these filthy wrecks? One of the three stepped forward.

"My name is Shackleton" he said.

"...if I am in the devil of a hole an want to get out of it, give me Shackleton every time."

Cherry-Garrard,
(who travelled with Captain Scott in 191

"For qualities of leadership, ability to organize, courage in the face of danger...Shackleton must be ranked as the first explorer of his age."

Frank Wild,
(who went on all Shackleton's expeditions)

"I had a very keen desire to see more of...the Antarctic snows and glaciers...the stark polar lands grip the hearts of the men who have lived on them."

Shackleton

Why was Shackleton a hero?

Shackleton was a determined and adventurous Irishman, and the Antarctic had cast its spell over him. In 1901 he had sailed to Antarctica with Captain Scott. Shackleton was a great leader who always took care of his men. His men trusted him completely. They called him "The Boss", and "Old Cautious". In 1907 he led his own expedition to the South Pole, but turned back rather than risk the lives of his team.

In August 1914, aged 40, he set out on his greatest expedition: the aim was to be the first team of men to cross the Antarctic continent on foot. But by the time the polar winter of 1914 closed in, Shackleton and his men had disappeared.

▲ Sir Ernest Shackleton (1874 - 1922). He was strong, not tall, with dark brown hair. With his firm chin and grey-blue eyes he looked a determined character.

The world gave them up for dead. Then, two years later, Shackleton "came back from the dead". The story of his survival, and the survival of his men, has become an Antarctic legend.

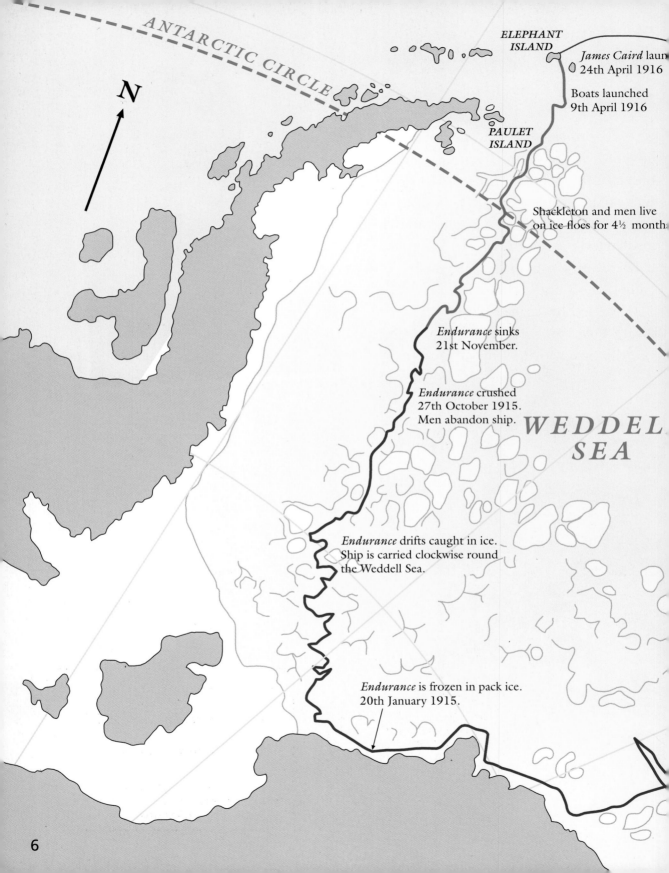

ANTARCTIC CIRCLE

N

ELEPHANT
ISLAND

James Caird laun
24th April 1916

Boats launched
9th April 1916

PAULET
ISLAND

Shackleton and men live
on ice floes for 4½ month

Endurance sinks
21st November.

Endurance crushed
27th October 1915.
Men abandon ship.

WEDDEL
SEA

Endurance drifts caught in ice.
Ship is carried clockwise round
the Weddell Sea.

Endurance is frozen in pack ice.
20th January 1915.

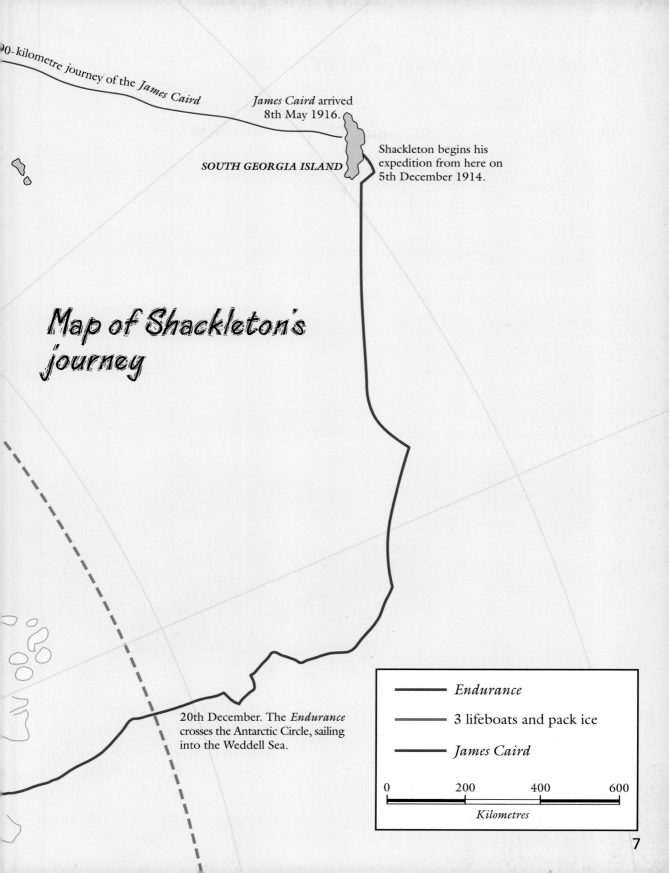

00-kilometre journey of the *James Caird*

James Caird arrived
8th May 1916.

SOUTH GEORGIA ISLAND

Shackleton begins his
expedition from here on
5th December 1914.

Map of Shackleton's journey

20th December. The *Endurance*
crosses the Antarctic Circle, sailing
into the Weddell Sea.

——	*Endurance*
——	3 lifeboats and pack ice
——	*James Caird*

0   200   400   600

Kilometres

Shackleton's ship Endurance

The Original Plan for the Imperial Trans-Antarctic Expedition

• *Two ships, the Endurance and the Aurora, will sail to Antarctica, one to each side of the* **ice cap** *that makes up that continent.*

• *The Aurora will sail down to the Ross Sea. The team from that ship will cross the ice half way, to the South Pole, laying camps and stores for Shackleton's team on the second half of their journey.*

• *The Endurance will sail down the opposite side of Antarctica with Shackleton and his men who will begin the crossing from that side.*

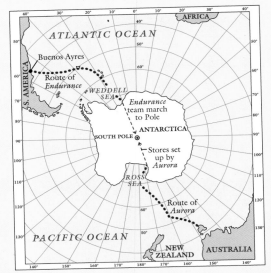

▲ The *Endurance* was specially built in Norway of pine and oak. Her strong bows could ram **ice floes** a metre thick, and split them.

1st August 1914:
THE EXPEDITION SETS SAIL ...

The First World War began just after Shackleton's ship, the *Endurance*, left London; but the expedition was told to carry on. This was to be the greatest pola journey ever – a march of nearly 3000 kilometres across the Antarctic ice cap.

Twenty-seven men sailed with Shackleton on the *Endurance*. There were 17 sailors and 10 others, including a photographer, an artist, scientists and doctors. They also took 69 dogs to pull sledges on the march.

Shackleton had chosen 56 men from 5000 **applicants**. He made up his mind about a man very quickly. Frank Worsley applied to be ship's captain because he said he had dreamed that he was steering a ship through ice, down a London street! Next morning, he went out and found the actual street, saw Shackleton's office and went in. Five minutes later, Shackleton hired him. Worsley's skill as a **navigator** was to save their lives.

▲ Shackleton's 1914 team

▲ The *Endurance* under full sail in the pack ice

In South Georgia the ship took on a tonne of whale meat for the dogs. The whalers there warned Shackleton that the ice that year looked as if it would be extremely dangerous. The *Endurance* sailed into the **pack ice**, which Shackleton called "nature's jigsaw puzzle". The pack ice got thicker, but the *Endurance* sailed on, crossing the Antarctic Circle on 20th December 1914.

5th November 1914:
THE ENDURANCE REACHES SOUTH GEORGIA ...

The pack ice closes in

Just as the whalers had predicted, Shackleton met **pack ice** earlier than he had expected. During December they made good progress, sailing 800 km through the loose pack ice. The ship coped well, driving a path through thin "leads" of clear water between the floating pack, or ramming **ice floes** to break them up.

Shackleton made sure the men kept cheerful. They played football on the ice, or hunted penguins to provide fresh food. Despite the fact that it was midsummer in Antarctica, on Christmas Day a freezing gale raged round the ship, but the men were snug below deck. They opened presents from home, and had a Christmas feast.

▲ Men hacked and sawed through the ice to make a path for the ship.

In January, making progress became harder. Huge, blue icebergs loomed dangerously close. The pack ice grew so thick that it took hours to move the ship a few yards.

▼ The pack ice in the Antarctic is like a jigsaw puzzle.

20th January 1915
ENDURANCE IS TRAPPED IN THE ICE …

▲ The Midwinter dinner

In May, Shackleton wrote: "We said goodbye to the Sun and entered midwinter twilight." They **celebrated** Midwinter's Day, 22nd June, with a special meal, but their food was getting short. In mid-July faint sunlight returned, but the weather got worse. **Blizzard** winds over 110 kph howled, and the temperature fell below −30°C.

The ice was never still. Huge pressure forced the ice floes together. The men heard the grinding noise against the sides of the ship as they slept. Through September and October, the pressure on the ship continued to increase. How long could the *Endurance* last?

The temperature fell sharply, to −23°C, so that the whole sea froze. The ship was stuck fast. One man described it as "frozen, like an almond in the middle of a chocolate bar."

Shackleton knew that they would be stuck all winter. The dogs were taken off the ship to live in ice kennels (they called them "dogloos"). Shackleton put some men in charge of training the dogs to pull sledges. Others hunted and killed all the seals they could find, to build up a stock of frozen meat.

▼ Taking the dogs out for exercise

January – October 1915
ENDURANCE DRIFTS 1800 KILOMETRES NORTH ...

The end of the Endurance

The men felt as if the ship was being squeezed to death. Her **timbers** shook and cracked like pistol shots. The iron plates of the engine room floor buckled and twisted. The ship was leaking badly, and teams of men exhausted themselves pumping icy water out of her.

They could not beat the ice. With the decks breaking up under them, Shackleton told his men "She's going boys, I think it's time to get off."

> "Her very sides opened and closed again as she was bent along her length, groaning.."
>
> Shackleton

The next stage of the fight for survival was beginning. Shackleton had already experienced the conditions in the Antarctic, and he was perhaps the only one who knew how hard a struggle they were facing.

▼ While millions of tonnes of ice were crushing the *Endurance*, the men **salvaged** as much of the equipment and supplies as possible.

27th October 1915:
SHACKLETON'S TEAM ABANDONS SHIP AND CAMPS ON THE ICE ...

▲ The *Endurance* sank in 10 minutes.

▼ The men huddled round the stove to keep warm.

The crew camped on an **ice floe** near their crippled ship. Their first ice floe was of newly made, thin ice that cracked under them. All night the men could hear killer whales **blowing** as they hunted for prey. They moved to a safer, stronger ice floe, which they called Ocean Camp, and rescued as many supplies as they could from the ship. They salvaged food, wood, ropes and metal to build a stove. They had tents, sleeping bags, ten sledges and three wooden lifeboats. All 28 men found themselves a new set of warm clothing.

The shout came "She's going boys!" as the **stern** of the *Endurance* rose and she nose-dived beneath the ice. In ten minutes the ice had closed over her. Their last link with home was gone.

"She's gone, boys," Shackleton said quietly. To cheer everyone up he organized a special treat for supper – fish paste and biscuits. But his entry in the **log** that night was short: "I cannot write about it."

21st November 1915:
THE ENDURANCE SINKS ...

How Shackleton took care of his men

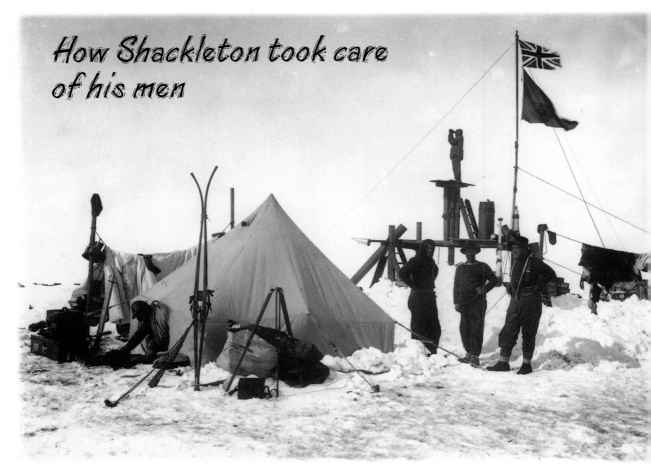

▲ Shackleton *(on the right)* in Ocean Camp. They had salvaged all the equipment they could from the Endurance.

Shackleton's plan was to drift along on the **ice floe** until they were near to Paulet Island which was about 550 km from the *Endurance*. Then they would row to the island. He knew there were stores of food there.

Shackleton knew the characters of his men. He carefully chose the groups who shared tents, to make sure that a bully, or a grumbler, did not cause others trouble. He planned celebrations for special days like Christmas Day and Midsummer's Day, which falls on 21 December in the Antarctic. He had to help his men fight cold and hunger, but he also knew they had to fight fear and boredom.

They had enough food to last 28 men three months. But by early December they were still nearly 500 km from Paulet Island.

November and December 1915
THE PARTY DRIFTS NORTH ON AN ICE FLOE...

Would their food last?

Shackleton reduced the daily rations, and made sure they caught as many seals and penguins as possible, to add to their supplies of meat, fat and oil. Then he took another hard decision. They could not waste their seal meat on the dogs. So, keeping some dogs for the sledge teams, he ordered the rest to be shot. The men who had trained and looked after the dogs were very upset.

"Grus is a fine little dog ... I have had him, fed him and trained him since he was born. I remember taking him out when he was a puppy in my pocket, only his nose peeping out ..."

Macklin, the doctor

▲ Frank Wild with his dogs

To speed up their journey, they tried to walk across the ice floes. Dogs pulled the sledges while the men hauled the boats. It was very hard work, and the going was painfully slow. It took them seven days to go 11 kilometres. At that rate it would take them 300 days to reach their goal – and they only had 42 days' food! Shackleton decided to stay put on the drifting ice.

▲ The men had to pull the boats across the ice, while the dogs pulled the sledges.

January 1916
THE MEN GIVE UP WALKING AND CAMP AGAIN...

Fighting Hunger

Daily food ration

Breakfast: 8oz sealmeat and tea *(250g)*
Lunch: 4oz biscuit and hot milk *(125g)*
Supper: 3/4 pint of seal stew *(400ml)*

▲ The sea-leopard is a fierce seal with sharp teeth and a spotted hide.

▲ There were plenty of crab-eater seals to boost their supplies.

Shackleton was saving their dry food for the boat journey ahead, so they hunted seals. The cook used the seal's fat, or **blubber**, as a cooking fuel. As the men got hungrier they ate strips of fried blubber. Later, in winter they even forced themselves to drink the thick black, smelly seal oil, to give them more energy.

January – April 1916
THE TEAM STAY AT PATIENCE CAMP ...

The men were hunted too. To some Antarctic animals, a man looked rather like their normal prey. A three-metre long sea-leopard attacked one man. Wild, Shackleton's second-in-command, shot it. There was constant danger from killer whales, which could swim up under an **ice floe** and tip seals into the water, and might do the same to the men.

Drifting helplessly

Blizzards and gales kept the men prisoners in their flimsy tents. They played cards and read, but sometimes they got on each others' nerves. Some doubted they would ever reach land.

The men thought about food all the time. By late March the daily ration was down to seal meat, blubber and dried milk. Drinking water was a problem.

"A bug on a single molecule of oxygen in a gale of wind would have about the same chance of predicting where he was likely to finish up."

James, the expedition scientist

▼ Waiting at Patience Camp, Ernest Shackleton (right) and Frank Hurley (left), who was the expedition's chief photographer.

FACT BOX

Drinking water is vital for survival. But you need to melt a bucketful of snow to make enough water for a mug of tea.

A man could fill a tobacco tin with ice and sleep with it next to his body to melt it and provide himself with a couple of spoonsful of water in the morning.

At the beginning of April, they shot the last two dog teams and ate them.

After he realized that they had drifted past Paulet Island, Shackleton decided their last chance of safety would be Elephant Island, but the ice floe they were on was starting to crack and break up. When it finally broke into pieces, would there be enough open water to launch the boats?

April 1916
THE ICE FLOE BEGINS TO BREAK UP ...

The end of Patience Camp

The boats were packed, and everyone ate a hot meal. At 11.00 a.m. the **ice floe** cracked apart under their feet. Launching the boats quickly, the crews rowed hard to get clear of the **pack ice**. Huge masses of tilting, tipping ice sent up enormous waves that nearly swamped them.

At 8.00 p.m. they pitched camp on another large ice floe. Shackleton kept watch. In the middle of the night, a crack opened up under a tent. Hearing cries, Shackleton saw a shape struggling in the water. It was someone in a sleeping bag. Reaching down, Shackleton hauled him up onto the ice. Seconds later the two edges of ice came together with a booming thud, just where the man had been. Everyone spent the rest of the night standing up, huddled together on the floe. They were still 160 kilometres from Elephant Island.

▼ Shackleton hauled the struggling man onto the ice, just in time.

9th April 1916
THE ICE BREAKS UP AND THEY TAKE TO THE BOATS ...

▲ After the ice floe broke up, the men took to the boats. At night, the boats were tied together for safety.

▲ A killer whale in icy seas

All next day they spent just floating, trapped by ice. With killer whales **blowing** all around, the towering icebergs threatened to crush them. That night the men lay in the boats, hugging each other for warmth.

"I do not think I had ever before felt the anxiety that belongs to leadership quite so keenly."
Shackleton

Next morning their eyes were red, salt and frost encrusted their faces, and their lips were cracked with thirst. They rowed and sailed towards Elephant Island. When night fell, the boats were tied together on the open sea. Sleep was impossible: a gale was blowing in sub-zero temperatures. The crew **bailed** all night, and chipped sea-ice off the boats. Shackleton did not think they would all survive the night.

AT SEA, THE CREW HAVE NO SLEEP OR HOT FOOD FOR 108 HOURS ...

Dry land at last!

At last they reached Elephant Island, and ate and slept at the foot of cliffs. Shackleton had to find a safer site. Wild volunteered to take a party and sail down the coast, where he found a long **spit** of stony land, sticking out into the sea.

▲ The route taken by the expedition, from South Georgia to the mainland of Antarctica, and back via Elephant Island

▲ The penguins on Elephant Island provided them with fresh food.

> "The health and mental state of several men were causing me anxiety"
> Shackleton

The whole party moved there next day. It was safe from high tides, but there was no shelter. The **blizzards** blew their big tent to shreds on the first night. But there were elephant seals and penguins nearby, so at least there was fresh food.

15th April 1916:
A SAFE LANDING ON ELEPHANT ISLAND ...

Many of the men were now very weak. The salt water had brought up boils on their skin. Many had **frostbite**. They only had five weeks' food left. They knew that the animals would leave the area when winter came, so there would be no more fresh meat. Worst of all, no one would come looking for them on Elephant Island as nobody would know they were there.

The voyage to South Georgia

▲ Crew of the *James Caird:* Ernest Shackleton (The Boss), Frank Worsley (**navigator**), Harry McNeish (carpenter), Thomas Crean, Timothy McCarthy, John Vincent.

Shackleton knew their only hope was to sail to the whaling stations on South Georgia. This meant sailing 1300 km across the Southern Ocean, which is the fiercest sea in the world. Waves 15 m high, and 1500 km wide, roll at 45 kph round the entire globe.

A small party of six set out in the *James Caird*, the boat they had fitted out specially for the dangerous voyage ahead.

They took sleeping bags, spare clothes, 30 days' food, water, oil for the small stove, and seal oil. Shackleton put Wild in charge of the 22 men left behind on Elephant Island.

▼ The design of the *James Caird*

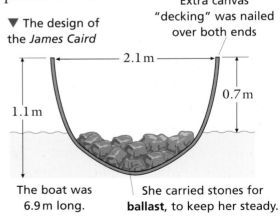

Extra canvas "decking" was nailed over both ends

2.1 m

1.1 m

0.7 m

The boat was 6.9 m long.

She carried stones for **ballast**, to keep her steady.

Dear Sir, in the event of my not surviving the boat journey...you will do your best for the rescue of the party....I have every confidence in you...you can convey my love to my people and say I tried my best."

(Shackleton's letter, left with Wild)

24th April 1916:
THE BOAT "JAMES CAIRD" IS LAUNCHED ...

An epic sea voyage

For 17 days the crew aboard the *James Caird* battled against hurricane winds and freezing seas. They had no oilskins to wear, only the wool and cotton clothes they had been in for seven months. Their skin was rubbed raw, and their hands were frost-bitten.

When they were not on their four-hour **watch**, they **bailed**, or crawled into their sodden, freezing sleeping bags. Their bodies ached from being thumped on the **ballast** stones as the tiny boat bucketed over huge waves.

Daily food ration

8.00 a.m.: hot "hoosh" (a nourishing soup Shackleton invented himself, made from lard, oatmeal, beef extract, salt and sugar),
2 biscuits,
lumps of sugar

1.00 p.m.: dry food and hot milk (made from milk powder)

5.00 p.m.: same again

night-time: hot drink

Shackleton protected the weaker men, but did not let them know it.

"He seemed to keep a mental finger on each man's pulse... if he noted one with signs of strain... he would order hot milk and soon all would be swallowing the life-giving drink to the especial benefit of the man, all unaware, for whom it had been ordered."

Worsley

FIFTEEN DAYS AT SEA IN ICY STORMS ...

Worsley's skill as a navigator

Worsley tried to use the Sun to chart their course – but he only saw it four times in 15 days. In between he worked out their course by a system called **"dead reckoning"**.

For the first five days they battled with gales. The seawater breaking over the boat froze, so the men had to hack ice off the boat. By day seven Worsley reckoned they were half way to South Georgia. The Sun came out, and everyone's hopes were raised: perhaps they would make it.

But day eleven brought the worst gale yet. At midnight, Shackleton saw a line of light in the sky. "It's clearing," he called. Then he realized the "light" was the crest of the biggest wave he had ever seen. "For God's sake hold on! It's got us!" he shouted. Amazingly, the tiny boat managed to stay afloat, full of water. The crew **bailed** water for their lives.

Their energy was sinking. Worsley said later, that he was sure some of the men would have given up and died, if Shackleton had not looked after them, and encouraged them not to abandon hope.

▼ Worsley's navigation instruments were like this.

4th May 1916:
THE BOAT IS SWAMPED BY A GIANT WAVE ...

Landing on South Georgia

When they saw South Georgia, Shackleton told them "the job was nearly done." But the ocean was not going to let them go easily. The very worst **hurricane** they had ever known blew up. For nine hours Worsley steered a zig-zag course, to stop them from being wrecked on the island's cliffs.

Everyone was exhausted, and very thirsty. "Most of us had the feeling that the end was very near," Shackleton wrote later. By daybreak, the hurricane had gone, but they took all day to find a landing place. The crew stumbled onto the beach, too weak to stand. Their frost-bitten limbs were cramped after crouching for 15 days.

Thanks to Worsley's seamanship, and Shackleton's leadership, the six of them had survived an **epic** journey.

Worsley wrote about "the Boss":

Being a born leader, he had to lead in the position of the most danger, difficulty and responsibility. I have seen him turn pale, yet force himself into the post of greatest peril...he would do the job that he was most afraid of."

7th May 1916:
SOUTH GEORGIA IS IN SIGHT ...

24

▲ At Cave Cove Shackleton held on to the boat all night.

The men unloaded the boat, but were too weak to pull it out of the water. They all needed rest and a meal. They found a cave, and slept. While his men were asleep, Shackleton hung on to the boat's rope, to stop it being washed away.

Next morning, they lined the cave floor with grass and put their sleeping bags round the fire. Nearby they found baby albatrosses, sitting tamely on their nests. They soon went into a stew which everyone agreed was delicious!

Exhausted, they slept deeply. In the middle of the night, Worsley woke up to ask if anyone could smell burning, because his feet were hot. No, they told him. It must just be his **frostbite** hurting, he thought, and went back to sleep. Next morning, he found a large hole burnt in his sleeping bag. Burning grass had set fire to it in the night!

Shackleton realized they could not stay in their cave for long. All the whaling stations were on the other side of South Georgia. His group was too weak to try and row and sail round the island, but the other party left on Elephant Island would not survive another winter. Shackleton decided they would have to walk across the island. "We must push on somehow," he said.

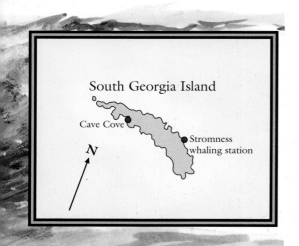

South Georgia Island

Cave Cove

Stromness whaling station

N

8th May 1916:
THE PARTY LANDS ON THE WRONG SIDE OF SOUTH GEORGIA ...

The final march

For nearly a week the men ate well and rested. Shackleton knew they could not march to the whaling stations until they got some strength back. But he never stopped thinking of the 22 people left on Elephant Island. They were his men, and he felt responsible for them

The party moved to a safer campsite because McNeish and Vincent were still very weak.

Leaving McCarthy to look after them, Shackleton, Crean and Worsley set off. Once again, they were facing unknown dangers. They had to find a way across to the other side of the island, to the whaling station in Stromness Bay. This would take them over an unmapped mountain range, with peaks 1500 m high.

They took three days food, a small stove, 48 matches, a sharp carpenters' tool as an ice axe, and 15 m of rope. Worsley also had a compass to chart their course.

▼ It was hard to find a safe route to the whaling station on the other side of the island.

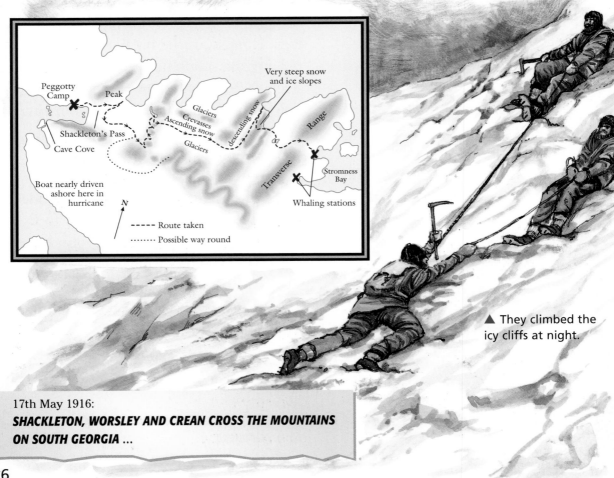

Peggotty Camp
Peak
Very steep snow and ice slopes
Glaciers
Crevasses
Ascending snow
descending snow
Range
Shackleton's Pass
Cave Cove
Glaciers
Transverse
Stromness Bay
Boat nearly driven ashore here in hurricane
N
Whaling stations
- - - - - Route taken
· · · · · · · Possible way round

▲ They climbed the icy cliffs at night.

17th May 1916:
SHACKLETON, WORSLEY AND CREAN CROSS THE MOUNTAINS ON SOUTH GEORGIA ...

Where sleep means death

The three of them left in clear moonlight, and by daybreak they were 900 m up the cliffs. They climbed, roped together, with Shackleton insisting on leading through the dangerous ice slopes and **crevasses**.

Twice they climbed to the top, only to find they had missed Stromness Bay. Each time they marched back down, then up again another way. After 16 hours, at the top again, they saw fog coming. They had to get down fast before night and fog overtook them. They roped themselves together and sat down. Then they launched themselves into the darkness, hurtling down a 300-metre snow slope, screaming with fear and excitement. At the bottom, they ate hot food, and decided to keep marching all night.

▲ Terrified, they launched themselves down the snow slope in darkness.

They kept on the move all night, because they had no sleeping bags. After 30 hours they rested, huddled together. Crean and Worsley instantly fell asleep. Shackleton, feeling his own eyes closing, shook himself awake. He knew that falling asleep meant they would all freeze to death. After five minutes, he shook the other two awake, telling them they had been asleep for half an hour.

20th May 1916:
7.00a.m. THE MEN HEAR THE WHISTLE FROM THE WHALING STATION ...

Rescued!

In the morning, about 1000 m below them, they saw the harbour. They cut steps down an ice cliff, waded across a frozen lake and down an icy waterfall. As they approached the whaling station, they realized how dreadful they must look.

Worsley wrote:

"Ragged, filthy, evil-smelling… unwashed for three months, no change of clothes for seven months…"

20th May 1916
STROMNESS WHALING STATION …

▲ Below them was Stromness whaling station, but the men still had to descend an icy cliff, cross a frozen lake and get through a waterfall.

Despite their appearance, they were met with relief and joy once the whalers realized who they were. Shackleton asked "When was the war over?" and was amazed to hear that hundreds of thousands of men were still being killed. The travellers felt as if they were waking from a long sleep "to a world gone mad".

After tea and cakes, they bathed, had haircuts, and were given new clothes. The other whalers crowded round to shake Shackleton's hand and hear the story of their ordeal.

The mysterious fourth person

That night, the gales began again. The rescue party had crossed the mountains during the only three days of fine weather that winter. Yet lying at last in warm, dry beds, they were too comfortable to sleep.

Safe at last, each man told the others his secret thoughts. It turned out that they had all felt a mysterious "presence", as if a fourth person had been walking with them through the ice and snow.

Who on Earth is it?

Worsley was taken by steamer to pick up the three men on the other side of South Georgia. He had to explain who he was – they didn't recognize a clean Frank Worsley!

Organizing the final rescue

But for Shackleton, the worries were far from over. He began at once to plan the rescue of the 22 men on Elephant Island knowing that their supplies must be running very low. But he was determined to save every one of his men. It was to take much longer than he expected.

29

Back to Elephant Island

The men on Elephant Island had hoped for a quick rescue. But by the end of May, Frank Hurley wrote "All are resigned now, and anticipate wintering." Once the winter **pack ice** had Elephant Island in its grip, no boat could reach them. Nevertheless, Wild, Shackleton's faithful second-in-command, kept everybody's spirits up. Every day that clear sea showed between the ice floes, he called "Roll up your sleeping bags, boys; the Boss may come today."

They had made a shelter from the two boats. They turned them upside down, on rocks, and stretched canvas round them to keep the wind out. They cooked, ate, slept, and lived under these two boats for four-and-a-half months. By the time they were rescued, they had only four days' food left, and they had taken to eating seaweed and limpets.

▲ Shackleton rowed in to rescue his men.

May – August 1916:
SHACKLETON MAKES FOUR ATTEMPTS TO REACH THE 22 MEN LEFT ON ELEPHANT ISLAND …

Shackleton had to make four rescue attempts before he could get through a gap in the ice around the island. Seeing the steamer, Wild and his men lit a signal fire and waved furiously. Worsley and the Boss spotted the camp.

In half an hour, Shackleton reached the beach. He shouted anxiously "Are you all well?"

"We are all well, boss" came the cry, and three cheers.

▲ The survivors were given a heroes' welcome at Punta Arenas, in South America.

Shackleton was proud that no man ever died under his leadership, and he was proud of those who shared his risks. He had survived an **epic** journey, and his own heroism had inspired his men.

> "It was a privilege to me to have had under my command men who, through dark days and continuous danger, kept up their spirits and carried out their work."
>
> Shackleton

30th August 1916:
THE MEN ON ELEPHANT ISLAND ARE RESCUED AFTER BEING MAROONED FOR NEARLY 5 MONTHS ...

Glossary

applicant A person who applies for a job.

bail To scoop out water that has got into a boat.

ballast Heavy material put into a boat to keep it steady.

blizzard Severe snowstorm.

blowing (whales) Whales breathe out a jet of air and water through a hole on the top of their head.

blubber Fat of whale or seal.

celebrate To do something special on an important day.

crevasse Deep crack in rock or ice.

dead-reckoning Working out a ship's position by using the log and compass.

epic Famous heroic story.

frostbite Harm done to body by freezing temperatures.

hurricane Storm with violent wind.

icecap Permanent ice cover at North and South Poles.

ice floe Sheet of floating ice.

log (of ship) Written record of a ship's voyage.

marooned To be stuck in a place with no means of escape.

nautical mile Measure of distance at sea (one nautical mile = 1.8 km).

navigator Sailor whose job is to make sure the ship is going in the right direction.

pack ice Mass of pieces of ice floating in the sea.

salvage To save from destruction.

spit (of land) Long finger of land sticking out into the sea.

stern Back end.

timbers (ship's) Wood planking making up the ship's sides.

watch (on ship) Taking a turn to be on duty.

Index

Books for further reading

Ice Trap! Shackleton's Incredible Expedition by Meredith Hooper
published by Frances Lincoln

South by Ernest Shackleton
published by Robinson Publishing

The Endurance: Shackleton's legendary Antarctic expedition by Caroline Alexander
published by Bloomsbury Publishing

Endurance by Alfred Lansing
published by Weidenfeld and Nicolson

Shackleton's Captain: a biography of Frank Worsley, by John Thomson
published by Mosaic Press